GROWING THINGS

Ron Thomas and Jan Stutchbury

Illustrated by Sharyn Madder

Irwin Publishing
Toronto, Canada

We saw daffodils in the garden.

4

How do they grow?

Deep under the soil the bulbs wait.
They wait through all
of the winter months.

6

They wait for the spring sun
to warm the soil.
Then a shoot begins to grow.

Soil

Bulb

Roots

Roots spread out to gather food and water from the soil to feed the bulb.

8

The shoot reaches the top of the soil.

Buds form at the top of each shoot.

10

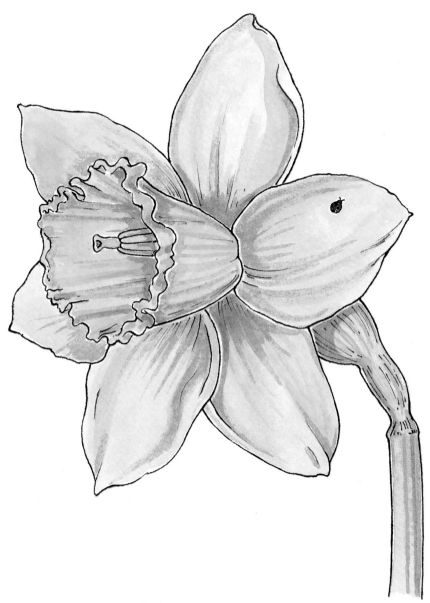

The daffodil blooms.

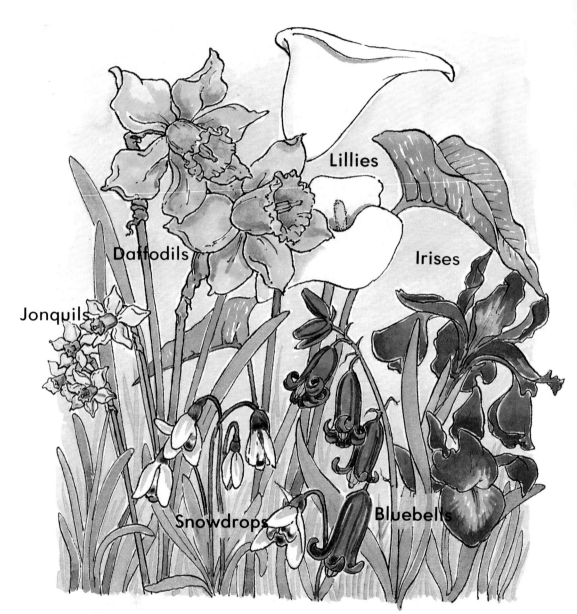

Lillies

Daffodils

Jonquils

Irises

Snowdrops

Bluebells

All of these flowers grow from bulbs.

12

New bulbs grow beside the old ones under the soil.
More daffodils will grow next year.

We grew bulbs at school.

15

Seeds

Plants grow from seeds.

16

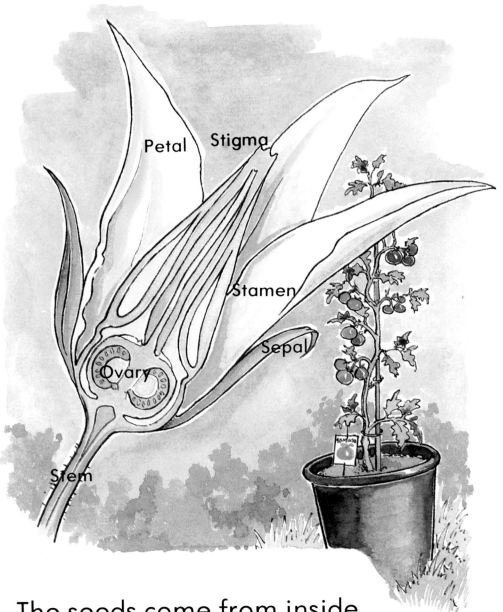

The seeds come from inside
the flower of a plant.

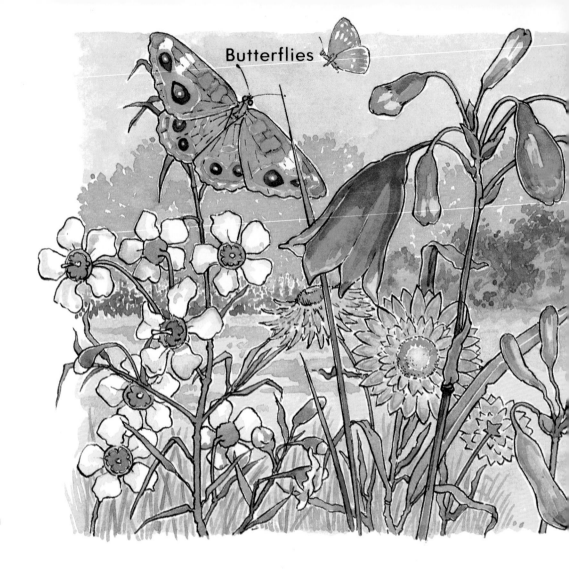

Butterflies

Seeds can only start to grow when
pollen from a flower touches
another flower.

18

Bees and other insects carry the
pollen from flower to flower.
Pollen can also be blown from
flower to flower by the wind.

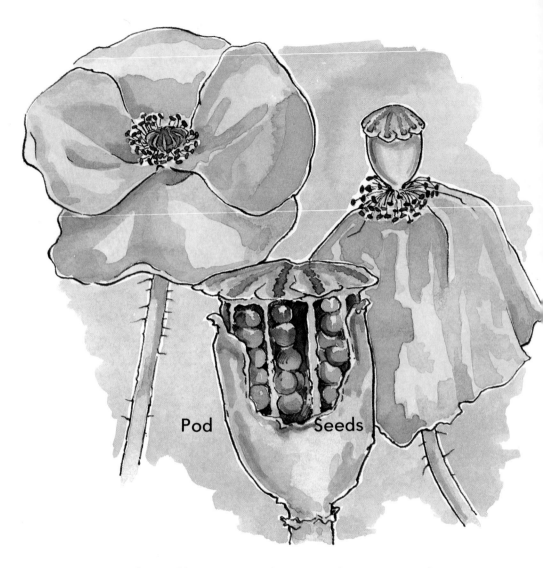

Pod   Seeds

When the flower dies, the seeds
keep growing inside pods
or in the fruit of the plant.

20

Pod

Seeds

Ripe fruit and pods break open
and the seeds fall to the ground.
New plants will grow.

Collecting
apple seeds

If I planted an apple seed . . .

22

Planting
apple seeds

One
year
later

Sapling

Five
years
later

apple
tree

Things you will need:
- jar
- soil
- bean seeds

1. Fill the pot with soil.

Soil

Jar

2. Push the bean seed down into the soil.

We planted some bean seeds like this.

3. Water it.

4. Leave the beans in
   a sunny spot and
   wait for them
   to root and shoot.

We watched them grow
into seedlings.

Seedlings

Then we planted the seedlings
into the soil in our garden.
We watered them and waited
for the flowers to grow.

26

Bean pods

Seeds

Soon the bean pods grew.
There were new seeds inside the pods.

When they were ripe we picked the
beans and ate some of them.
We kept some bean seeds to plant
next year.

Glossary

bee	bulb
daffodil	flower
fruit	planting

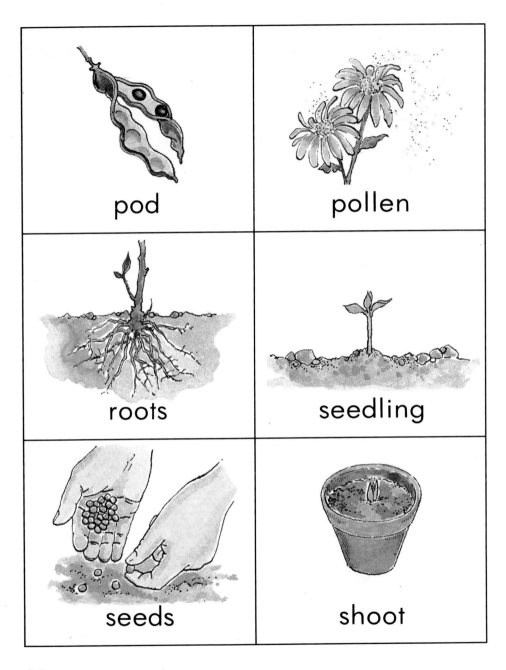

pod

pollen

roots

seedling

seeds

shoot